Spiders
For Kids

Amazing Animal Books
for Young Readers

by John Davidson

Mendon Cottage Books

JD-Biz Publishing

Read More Amazing Animal Books

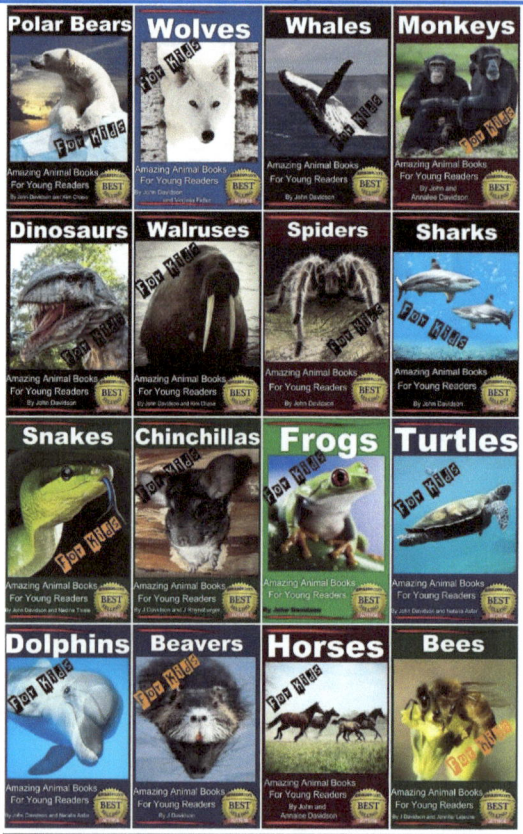

Purchase at Amazon.com

Download Free Books!
http://MendonCottageBooks.com

Table of Contents

Introduction to Spiders

Spiders are the most distributed of all the insects on earth. They are found in every part of the world except in Antarctica. 40,000 species of the spiders are found on earth. Introduction to spiders can be done by knowing about their anatomy. The body of the spider is divided into two parts. The upper part is called cephalothorax and the lower part is the abdomen. Spiders don't have antennae like other insects.

Spiders eat other spider and insects. They catch their prey by weaving web in which insects are caught. Large spiders eat lizard and birds.

They cannot eat solid food because their intestines are very narrow, so to digest their food spiders uses digestive enzymes on the food and have the liquid juices which are produced.

Many spiders are very poisonous. They attack their prey with the poison excreted by them. All the species of spiders don't sting. Spiders have glands which produce silk. These glands are in their abdomen.

10 Facts About Spiders

Are you one of the people who are afraid of spiders? Well, spiders frighten many people but on the other hand they have some interesting facts that you need to know.

1. Spiders are not insects; they have 8 legs while insects have 6. They belong to a group called arachnid. Ticks, scorpions and mites belong to this group also.

2. Spider silk is very strong and flexible. Some varieties are even 5 times stronger than steel of the same size.

3. Some are as huge as a dinner plate. The Goliath Bird-eater Tarantula from South America is 10-11 inches wide.

4. A species called raft spider can walk on water.

5. Cobwebs you find in the house are abandoned spider webs.

6. Spiders have up to 8 eyes which are used to distinguish between some species.

7. Some spiders can live up to 30 years though many die after a year or two.

8. Spiders don't have ears and use hairs on their legs to sense sound.

9. Some spit on their prey to catch them.

10. Spiders can jump almost 50 times more than their length.

Spider Eggs

Spider eggs are usually laid in unique egg sacks that are usually made of silken material. These sacs are usually ball-shaped, in most cases; they are carried by the female spiders or hidden in a less conspicuous area such as under the leaves, on branches or inside the web itself.

Nursery Web Spider with Her Eggs

For the egg to hatch into a newborn spider, it has to be fertilized by the male spiders. After the fertilization process, they are usually placed in a safe location away from other living organisms that can eat them. In fact, some of the spiders prefer carrying their eggs around until they hatch so as to ensure that the safety of their young ones is not compromised.

The young ones of a spider is referred to as spiderlings, they undergo a number of process until they reach the adult stage. Finally, note that scientists have being able to prove that some spiders can live for more than 20 years.

Spider Anatomy

Spiders have many characteristics that distinguish them from other animals. Some of the characteristics are:

The external anatomy of spiders

Their bodies are subdivided into 2 segments.

They have 8 jointed legs.

They do not have wings

They have no antennae.

They have simple eyes.

They have an exoskeleton. They periodically shed the exoskeleton.

In addition, it is important to remember that spiders have certain features that distinguish them from other arachnids.

The internal anatomy of spiders

Spiders have an open circulatory system. This means that their bodies are filled with a substance called haemolymph and therefore they have no blood vessels in their bodies. Their haemolymph has a substance called hemocyanin which is an equivalent hemoglobin in creatures like human beings. On the other hand, they have several respiratory anatomies. Generally, spiders are interesting animals to study and every pupil should be ready to learn and discover more about this creatures.

Spider Habitat

Did you know that spiders are found on every continent except Antarctica? It is too cold there for them to survive. They live just about everywhere. Even where there is no water around at all. They can survive in just about any condition.

Tropical areas have many different types of spiders. They can find lots of food to enjoy and have many places to build their nests. When it gets cooler out they have to find a warmer place to live or they will die. That is why you do not seem them in the winter when it is cold out.

Agelena labyrinthica – male

It can be hard to spot where spiders live if you do not look carefully. They blend into their surroundings very well and do not come out of their hiding spots too often. Many spiders can be found living near water like wetlands. They do not need the water to drink; instead, they find lots of food and shelter nearby. This is a very popular spot for them. So is the inside of your house. If you look carefully you will find them all over your house inside and out.

Spider Silk

A spider silk basically refers to a fiber that has been spun by the spiders and is protein in nature. It is used by the spiders for making spider webs and other structures. The web is then used to protect their young ones and also for trapping other animals. The silk can also be used by the spiders for suspending themselves.

Formation

The process by which the spiders use in the formation of silk is through spinning. Silk proteins are released from by some special glands after which they are dissolved in a water based solution. The solution is then pushed outside through the ducts where they stretch to form long strands which are then wound to form the silk.

Unlike other insects whereby an individual produces only one silk, one spider can produce around seven unique types of silk each with different uses.

Other uses

Silk is also used by spiderlings when they during dispersal for ballooning. The type used for ballooning is an extremely fine one and is referred to as gossamer. The ballooning exercise is achieved by extruding a number of threads to the open air and then allowing themselves to be swung by the winds. They may not be carried far though but this is the main method that they use to disperse. Sometimes, the spiders use the silk as a source of food especially when the food is scarce and the competition is high.

Aside from the basic functions to which the silk is intended to perform, it has greatly been beneficial to humans. Spider silk is one of the toughest materials that is used for various purposes such as dress making, making fishing lines among others.

Spider Webs - For Catching Prey

Spider webs are made by spiders. These webs are found in the corners of old homes. The existence of the web is nearly 100 million years old.

Spider webs which are made perfectly are a masterpiece of beauty. Spider makes these webs to catch their prey. As these webs are sticky the insects are caught in it. These insects provide nutrition to the spider.

After making a new web, the spiders eat up their old web. The different types of spider webs are sheet webs, funnel webs, spiral webs, tangle webs and tubular webs. The silk which is used to make the spider webs are fluffy capture silk and sticky capture silk. The construction of these webs can be done in a horizontal plane, a vertical plane or in any other angle.

Every species of spiders don't build these webs and there are some who don't make these spider webs. Spider web is different from cobweb as cobweb is the web which is left by the spiders.

Spider Senses

Spiders lack good vision and they rely entirely on their senses. They have 4 pairs of eyes that are near sided. They can't see very far. What they see is dependent on the arrangement of the eyes. They can move their eyes in different directions in the same time. Spiders are capable of telling their direction by their eyes since they have poor sense of direction.

They create webs to enable them to escape easily and also catch their prey since they find it hard to move without the web. On the other hand, there are several species of spiders that have very sensitive nails in their feet. The nails help them to pick up different movements around them.

The sense of smell is strong in spiders. They use the sense in various situations like in finding mates. The reason why they bite humans is because of their senses. If you touch them by accident, a natural defense mechanism is triggered in the spider and they will bite since they sense danger.

Spider Bites

Spider bites can be defined as injuries that result from bites by spiders and other closely related arachnids. It is important to understand that a spider in an active hunter that relies heavily on its bites so as to paralyze and kill its prey. On the other hand, a spider will use bites as a mechanism for defense. Did you know that spiders rarely bite unless they are threatened? Spider bites will result in allergic reactions and that is why our bodies portray various symptoms when bitten by spiders.

Telling if a victim has been bitten by a spider is not easy especially if you have not attended a first aid class. If you are bitten by a spider, it is very likely that you will confuse the bite with that of a bee. Common reactions to spider bites will be symbolized by.

- Redness

- Pain as well as swellings on the site.

Types Of Spiders

There are around 40,000 types of spiders that can be found in different parts of the world. Some of the most common species of spiders that are found in our homes or surroundings are the:

Cellar spider

This is a common house spider. It is usually whitish or cream in color. This type of spider is not poisonous and usually feeds on pests that are mostly found within the household.

Cellar (House) Spider

Black widow spider

It is one of the most poisonous species of spiders in the world. It is black in color with red spots around the abdomen. It can be found in secluded corners and building under construction.

Black Widow

Cobweb spider

This type of spider is also referred to as the common house spider. It is mostly found indoors in damp and secluded areas. It is grayish and can also have a brownish color appearance. It loves constructing webs that help it move around.

Interestingly, not all species of spiders are poisonous, only a small number of species are.

Spider Identification

A spider is an air-breathing arthropod that has 8 legs. It also has chelicerae with fangs that inject poisonous substances called venom. Spiders are the biggest order of arachnids. They are found everywhere in the world except the continent of Antarctica.

Anatomically, a spider is completely different from several other arthropods because the segments of their bodies are fused into 2 tagmata i.e. the abdomen and the cephalothorax. The 2 body parts are joined together by a cylindrical pedicel. There are several species of spiders that can be found across the world. As a student, you should be willing to explore and identify the various types of spiders. You should also be able to tell the distinguishing features of a spider. Don't also forget that spiders have interesting internal anatomy like breathing, circulation and feeding.

In summary, the basic distinguishing features of a spider include:

- Two body parts

- No wings

- They have open circulatory system

Black Widow Spiders

The Black Widow is one of the most deadliest and venomous spiders and is the most venomous in the United States of America. The average lifespan of female black widow spider is between 9-15 months during which she may produces 700 offspring.

Black Widow

This species have the potential to kill a human within few hours. Generally only mature female Black Widow spider carries venom. The bite of male spider is not dangerous to human. Their venom attacks the victim's respiratory rate, nervous system and blood pressure. The venom of the black widow spider breaks down muscle, skin and also bone into a liquid so that they could digest. Instant death takes place if the spider strikes smaller prey. Like other spiders, the Black Widow Spider is nocturnal and hunts its prey during the evening hours. The females of this species are solid black in color while males are light brown with numerous tan markings.

Crab Spider

On this article we are going to be learning about a species of spiders referred to as the crab spider. Why the name crab spider? Well, that's simple. They physically resemble crabs. Their Front legs are at the same angle as those of crabs, and are also outstretched outwards. Another similarity that crab spiders have to crabs is that they can move in a forward, backward and sideways fashion.

Crab Spider

Crab spiders can literally be found throughout the world, meaning they adapt quite well to different climates. Most of them can be found on flowery or leafy environments lying in wait for their prey. Their diet mainly comprises of insects. Unlike most spiders, the crab spiders do not use webs to capture their prey but are instead known to ambush their prey. They are excellent at camouflage and use this to their advantage when hunting.

Crab spiders have a venomous bite that is not dangerous to humans. With that in mind, it is still not a good idea to mess around with them. There are some whose bite is awfully painful while bites from others will only leave you with a little discomfort.

Baby Spiders

Baby spiders are referred to as spiderlings. The spiderlings have no color at all and this is an adaptive characteristic that helps in protection from predators (animals that may feed on them).

Formation

Many baby spiders are born inside the sac from the egg. After they get out of the egg, they then form a strand of silk which help them float away.

When the hatching process is complete, they stay inside the sac until they have undergone the first moult after which they will emerge through a neat hole that they have cut out. They then form clusters together where they will largely be living on the yolk sac remains.

Dispersal

After some times (days or weeks) they begin to gradually disperse away so as to avoid food competition and also prevent themselves from being fed on by their siblings.

The different species types disperse differently with the burrowers and those dwelling on the ground walking over short distance. Others like the foliage dwellers & web builders disperse by ballooning and bridging.

Wolf Spider Babies

Although many may survive until after the dispersal stage, they are not free from the predators yet. Many of them therefore tend to continue staying in the communal web until they are mature enough to fend for themselves. During this time, they support themselves by feeding on their own web and also on the pollen that may be blown by the winds. They also take in the moisture condensed in the silk.

Brown Recluse Spiders

Brown recluse spiders are also called violin spiders. They have venomous bites. A standard-sized brown recluse spider measures approximately 6-20 mm, but they may even grow larger. As their name suggests they are light to medium brown in color though their color may also range from cream to blackish gray. In certain situations you may find one whose abdomen and cephalothorax are not of the same color. These types of spiders are normally characterized by marks on their dorsal sides of the cephalothorax. They species normally live up to 2 years

A major distinguishing characteristic is that they lower their bodies if alarmed, and then withdraw the forward 2 legs in a defensive position.

They standstill in a motionless position while keeping their pedipalps raised. Mature ones have dark pedipalps that are prominent and held forward horizontally.

With the above description, I hope you can picture this type of spider. It is important that you find a brown recluse spider that is live for you to clarify that. Remember to take caution since their bites are poisonous. Always seek assistance from a mature person.

Funnel Spider

A funnel spider is long and has an oval shape. They are black in color. It has long and thin legs. They also have small eyes. funnel web spiders eat snails, beetles, large insects and small animals. They are mainly found in grass, stones or at the corners of buildings. They can live for many years. Funnel spiders cannot see well and move by vibrations caused by objects. Funnel spiders are very poisonous. If you are in a place that has spiders, you should always check your shoes before you wear them. But if you do not disturb them, they will also not disturb you.

The female funnel spiders lays eggs. The eggs then hatch into young spiders. The young spiders are then raised in a burrow. The female funnel spiders then leave the burrow after some time and build their own burrow. The male spiders stay in their mother's burrow until they become adults. They then leave the burrow to look for a mate.

Tarantula Spiders

Tarantulas belong to the spider family. They also have 8 legs just like any other spider. One distinguishing feature that is interesting and different from other spiders is that they have very hairy legs and bodies. Their lifespan reaches up to 30 years. Unlike most other spiders the tarantulas do not spin webs. They catch their prey by fighting and pursuit.

It is interesting to know that there are over 800 species of tarantula. Their sizes may vary from one inch to as big as a foot. Mostly the tarantulas are black or brown in color. There are some species that have attractive colors like the Cobalt Blue Tarantula that has deep blue colored legs and the Mexican Red-Legged Tarantula that has bright red markings on their legs.

For several years now the tarantulas have been a relatively popular pet. Keeping tarantulas as pets can make a fascinating hobby as they are quiet and unique, and need little space. Out of all the exotic pets the tarantulas require very low maintenance. They can be trained quite well as pets as they are gentle.

Jumping Spiders

Jumping spiders are very common and they are found all over the world. They are even found in and around our houses. They are not at all harmful and you don't need to be scared of them at all.

They have been given this name as jumping spider because they can jump really well. They have very good eyesight also.

They are very easy to recognize. Simply look closely at the spider and if you see 2 large eyes and 2 smaller eyes on the face then you can make out that it is a jumping spider. Another thing to see is that the jumping spiders are usually very small. They are not big like the other spiders that we commonly read and learn about. If you see that the spider has bigger front 4 legs and the 4 legs at the back are small then you can be sure that the spider is a kind of a jumping spider.

World's Most Poisonous

According to research spiders have been found among the insects that are to harmful to human beings. However not all spiders are harmful and some have been named to be more dangerous than the others. The most dangerous spiders are the ones with very toxic venom that can cause a human being to be ill.

Brown Recluse Spider

Basically, the most dangerous venom spiders include funnel web and brown recluses spiders. The brown recluses are mainly found in the Northern America while funnel web are found in some areas in Australia. These spiders excrete very poisonous venom that can cause fatal sickness to human beings. This condition can mostly occur to small children, if bitten.

Another named world's dangerous spider is the Brazilian Wandering Spider. Research has found out that fatal bites rarely occur. They may be even less than 1% of all reported bites. If you happen to be bitten by a spider it's good to seek medical attention since it's hard to determine the less and most dangerous spiders.

Read More Amazing Animal Books

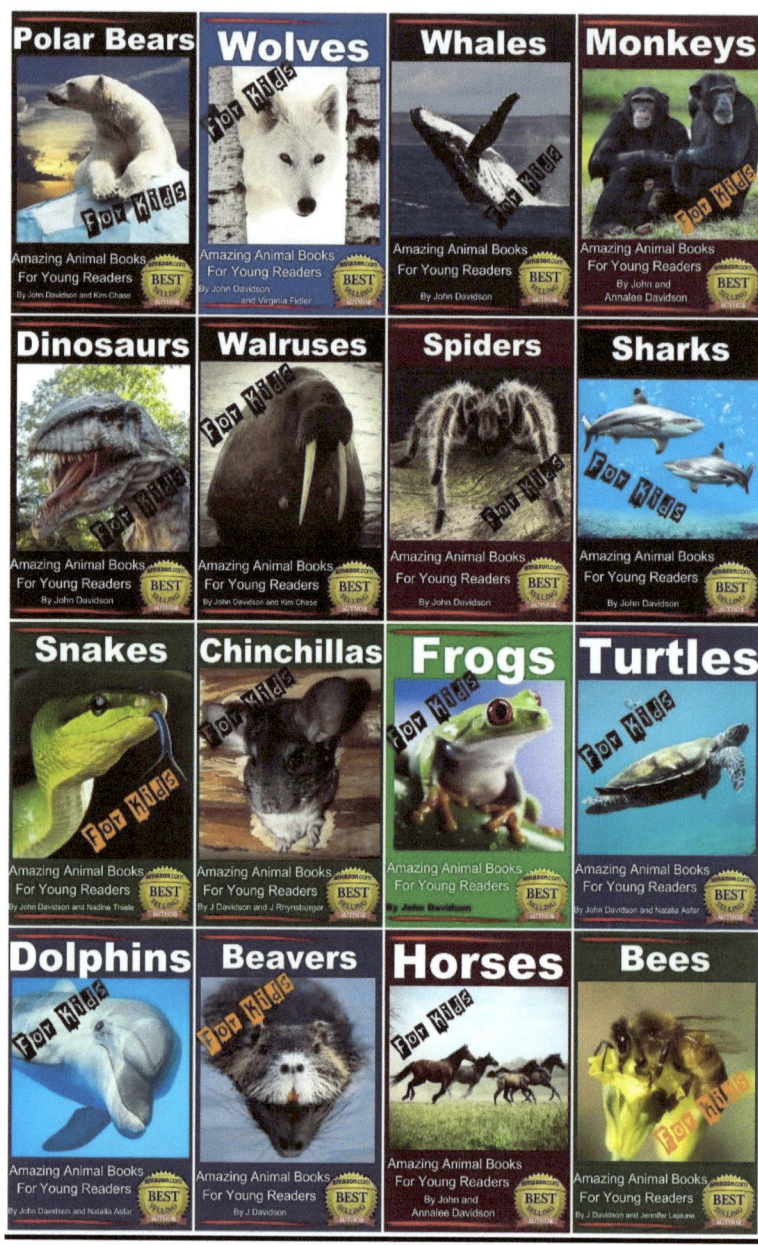

Purchase at Amazon.com
Website http://AmazingAnimalBooks.com

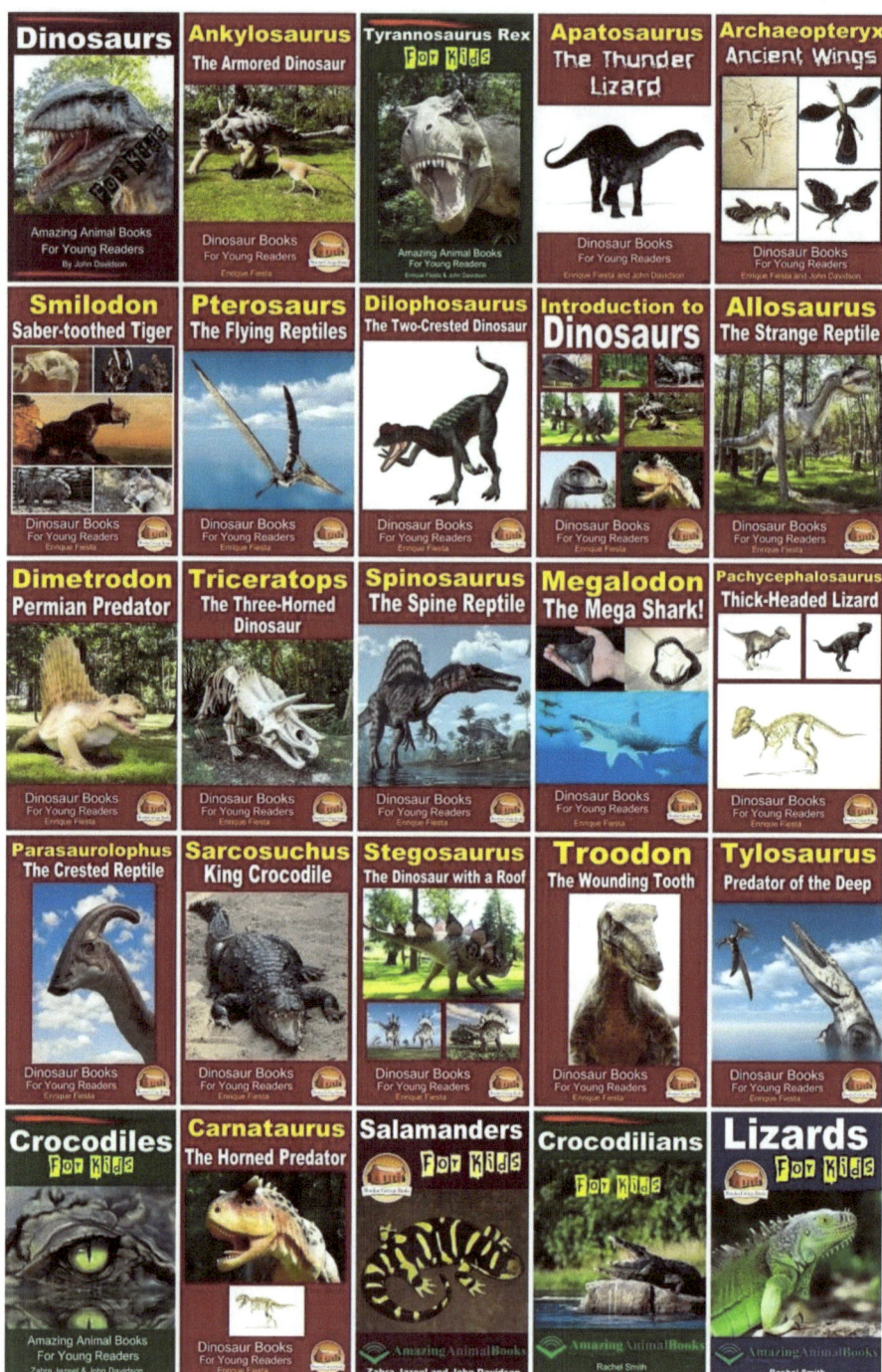

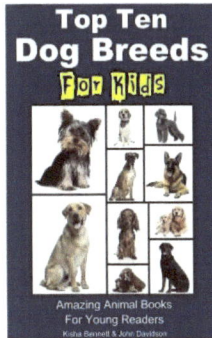

Top Ten Dog Breeds For Kids
Amazing Animal Books
For Young Readers
Kisha Bennett & John Davidson

German Shepherds
Dog Books for Kids
K. Bennett

Bulldogs
Dog Books for Kids
K. Bennett

Dachshund

Dog Books for Kids
K. Bennett

Poodles
Dog Books for Kids
K. Bennett

Labrador Retrievers
Dog Books for Kids
K. Bennett

Rottweilers
Dog Books for Kids
K. Bennett

Boxers
Dog Books for Kids
K. Bennett

Golden Retrievers
Dog Books for Kids
K. Bennett

Puppies
Dog Books For Kids
Amazing Animal Books
By John Davidson

Beagles
Dog Books for Kids
K. Bennett

Yorkshire Terriers
Dog Books for Kids
K. Bennett

Dogs
Top Ten Dog Breeds For Kids
Amazing Animal Books
For Young Readers
Zahra Jazeel & John Davidson

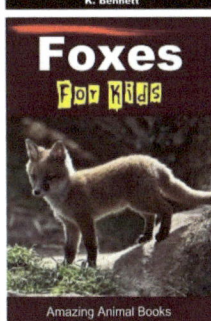

Cats For Kids
Amazing Animal Books
For Young Readers
K. Bennett & John Davidson

Foxes For Kids
Amazing Animal Books
For Young Readers
Zahra Jazeel & John Davidson

Wolves For Kids
Amazing Animal Books
For Young Readers
By John Davidson and Virginia Fidler

Our books are available at

1. Amazon.com
2. Barnes and Noble
3. Itunes
4. Kobo
5. Smashwords
6. Google Play Books

Download Free Books!
http://MendonCottageBooks.com

Publisher

JD-Biz Corp

P O Box 374

Mendon, Utah 84325

http://www.jd-biz.com/

Mendon Cottage Books

P O Box 374, Mendon Utah 84325

www.ingramcontent.com/pod-product-compliance
Lightning Source LLC
Chambersburg PA
CBHW050838290526
45792CB00001B/444